Q

APR 2016

Sportswriting and Sports Photography

CAREERS
OFF THE FIELD

CAREERS OFF THE FIELD

Sportswriting and Sports Photography

By John Walters

Mason Crest

450 Parkway Drive, Suite D
Broomall, PA 19008
www.masoncrest.com

Printed and bound in the United States of America.

Series ISBN: 978-1-4222-3264-4
Hardback ISBN: 978-1-4222-3273-6
EBook ISBN: 978-1-4222-8531-2

First printing
1 3 5 7 9 8 6 4 2

Produced by Shoreline Publishing Group LLC
Santa Barbara, California
Editorial Director: James Buckley Jr.
Designer: Bill Madrid
Production: Sandy Gordon
www.shorelinepublishing.com
Cover photo: Newscom: Mike Weyerhaeuser/ActionPlus

Library of Congress Cataloging-in-Publication Data is on file with the publisher.

CONTENTS

Key Icons to Look For

Words to Understand: These words with their easy-to-understand definitions will increase the reader's understanding of the text, while building vocabulary skills.

Sidebars: This boxed material within the main text allows readers to build knowledge, gain insights, explore possibilities, and broaden their perspectives by weaving together additional information to provide realistic and holistic perspectives.

Research Projects: Readers are pointed toward areas of further inquiry connected to each chapter. Suggestions are provided for projects that encourage deeper research and analysis.

Text-Dependent Questions: These questions send the reader back to the text for more careful attention to the evidence presented here.

Series Glossary of Key Terms: This back-of-the-book glossary contains terminology used throughout this series. Words found here increase the reader's ability to read and comprehend higher-level books and articles in this field.

Foreword
By Al Ferrer

So you want to work in sports? Good luck! You've taken a great first step by picking up this volume of CAREERS OFF THE FIELD. I've been around sports professionally—on and off the field, in the front office, and in the classroom—for more than 35 years. My students have gone on to work in all the major sports leagues and for university athletic programs. They've become agents, writers, coaches, and broadcasters. They were just where you are now, and the lessons they learned can help you succeed.

One of the most important things to remember when looking for a job in sports is that being a sports fan is not enough. If you get an interview with a team, and your first sentence is "I'm your biggest fan," that's a kiss of death. They don't want fans, they want pros. Show your experience, show what you know, show how you can contribute.

Another big no-no is to say, "I'll do anything." That makes you a non-professional or a wanna-be. You have to do the research and find out what area is best for your personality and your skills. This book series will be a vital tool for you to do that research, to find out what areas in sports are out there, what kind of people work in them, and where you would best fit in.

That leads to my third point: Know yourself. Look carefully at your interests and skills. You need to understand what you're good at and how you like to work. If you get energy from being around people, then you don't want to be in a room with a computer because you'll go nuts. You want to be in the action, around people, so you might look at sales or marketing or media relations or being an agent. If you're more comfortable being by yourself, then you look at analysis, research, perhaps the numbers side of scouting or recruiting. You have to know yourself.

You also have to manage your expectations. There is a lot of money in sports, but unless you are a star athlete, you probably won't be making much in your early years.

I'm not trying to be negative, but I want to be realistic. I've loved every minute of my life in sports. If you have a passion for sports and you can bring professionalism and quality work—and you understand your expectations—you can have a great career. Just like the athletes we admire, though, you have to prepare, you have to work hard, and you have to never, ever quit.

Series consultant Al Ferrer founded the sports management program at the University of California, Santa Barbara, after an award-winning career as a Division I baseball coach. Along with his work as a professor, Ferrer is an advisor to pro and college teams, athletes, and sports businesses.

Introduction

The Los Angeles Lakers play 41 regular-season home games each year at the Staples Center (left), and so do the Los Angeles Clippers. Arash Markazi, who covers both NBA teams as a writer for ESPN.com, attends nearly all of them.

"I grew up as a Los Angeles sports fan," says Markazi, 34, "and I got into this profession because I have a passion for sports. And don't get me wrong—I appreciate being at the games. But really, I just want to write a good story."

On this night, the Lakers are hosting the Sacramento Kings, but Markazi's day begins long before the 7:30 P.M. tip-off. At 9:30 A.M., he heads to the team's practice facility in El Segundo, California, to watch the pregame shootaround. The shootaround is an informal practice that basketball teams hold on the mornings of game days.

"The shootaround isn't a big deal normally," says Markazi, "but when you are covering a team, and especially at the speed with which news travels these days, you can't afford to not be there if something big does occur. Also, coaches and players tend to respect you more when they see that you are working as hard at your job as they are at theirs."

In South Bend, Indiana, photographer Matt Cashore's game-day preparation to shoot Saturday afternoon's Notre

Sports photographer Matt Cashore has a front-row seat for every event he attends . . . when he is working!

Dame football game begins in earnest on Friday evening. "It's a little like packing for a camping trip," says Cashore, who works for both the University of Notre Dame and for *USA Today's* **wire service**. "Will it rain? I'll have to pack rain gear to protect the cameras. How many cameras should I bring? It may be as few as three or as many as six."

For today's 3:30 P.M. kickoff against the University of North Carolina, Cashore arrives on campus at 10 A.M. He wants to take pictures of the Fighting Irish band marching across campus, so he positions himself in the second-floor window of the Law School, past which the band will march. Then he heads over to Notre Dame Stadium.

"There's so much to do before the game," says Cashore, "that the game itself is almost anticlimactic."

For instance, it is Cashore's responsibility to provide captions for each photo that he will upload to the wire service.

In order to do that, he uses a computer app called "Code Replacement" that affixes a code for every player involved in the game. That way Cashore can simply type in the code's digits instead of spelling out players' names each time.

"It's a time-consuming process," says Cashore, "but you don't want to be delayed sending in photo captions too long after you've taken the photos."

Back in Los Angeles, Markazi drives downtown after the shootaround. He spends a few hours in ESPN's offices. At least a few times per week, he appears as a guest on ESPN's Los Angeles sports radio station. Some days, he also appears on a short television segment for one of the ESPN networks to discuss the Lakers or Clippers or baseball's Los Angeles Dodgers, or even college teams such as the UCLA Bruins or USC Trojans.

"It might seem overwhelming at times," says Markazi, "but this is what I'm naturally interested in. It never feels like work."

For a night game, Arash likes to be inside Staples Center by 5 P.M. Years of experience have taught him that the best players, such as the Lakers' Kobe Bryant, prefer to take shooting practice on the floor at around this time, long before the fans are allowed inside the arena.

On the field at Notre Dame, Cashore positions himself in the south end zone and says a prayer of thanks that it is not raining. During each play he may take anywhere between 10 to 30 photos. He'll use either his Nikon D4-S with a telephoto lens that is mounted on a **monopod,** or an autofocus camera that is slung around his neck.

After almost every play, Cashore stares into his LCD viewfinder and deletes all but his favorite shots. This process is known as **chimping** and all sports photographers do it. It's another time-saving process.

"At halftime, I'll head into the photo work room inside the stadium and send my first batch of photos," says Cashore. "Chimping means that I've already edited my photos before halftime, so that all I have to worry about now is uploading them to my computer and sending them."

The back alleys of the Staples Center are a second home to Markazi, and the Lakers' staff and security know him well. He is a naturally **affable** person, which he finds is an invaluable trait in his job. "Just talking to people, whether it be the twelfth man on the Lakers' bench or John Black [the long-time media relations director of the Lakers] does a few things for you," Markazi says.

"First, it lets them see you are a real person. Also, it builds trust. I may talk to Nick Young about where he'll want to go to dinner when the Lakers play in New Orleans. That's not a basketball conversation, but it helps build a rapport between us."

Arash Markazi (left) has watched the Lakers win three of these NBA championship trophies.

During the game Markazi sits on press row, an area reserved for members of the media. In large markets such as Los Angeles, press row is actually behind one of the baskets and a few rows back. At any time during the game, or even throughout the day, Markazi may field a phone call, text message, or email from an ESPN editor asking him to file a quick story. It may concern the Lakers, but it just as often may concern something else related to Los Angeles sports.

"I like to work on longer features," Markazi says, "but a three hundred-word story that receives just as many clicks online is just as valuable and takes far less time."

In fact, the previous day on ESPN Los Angeles, the most heavily read story was a brief report about Kobe Bryant recently having breakfast with Rajon Rondo of the Boston Celtics. "What did they discuss?" Markazi asks. "Nobody knows. Did they say, 'Pass the salt?' But I still had to write about it."

Back inside Notre Dame Stadium, the Fighting Irish are putting the finishing touches on a 50–43 win. Cashore readies himself to run onto the field for the postgame handshakes. He wants to shoot "celebration or dejection photos," as he calls them, but he does not want to linger on the field too long.

"After the game, you want to get back to the work room and upload your photos," says Cashore. "There is

Cashore, kneeling at bottom left, uses a short lens for close-up work. He keeps the long lens for action shots across the field.

a race among photographers to be the quickest to get a picture out to the wider world."

In Los Angeles, the Lakers win 98–95, and Markazi files a quick "gamer" that ESPN can post immediately. During the game, he has been typing paragraphs as the action takes place, and it's finished right after the game ends. This first story is valued not for its style, but because it is available right away.

Once that piece is filed, Markazi heads to the locker rooms to interview players and coaches. By 10:30 P.M. he will be seated in front of his computer once again, crafting a longer and more detailed story that will then be sent to an ESPN editor in Los Angeles or Chicago or Bristol, Connecticut. By midnight, with any luck, Markazi will be finished.

Sportswriter and sports photographer both pack a lot of work into long days. Markazi and Cashore devote 10 to 12 hours—or more—on game days to perform their duties. "Nobody sees the process of what we do," says Cashore. "It's far more time-consuming than the game itself."

For people who love to tell stories about sports, however, there is no better job in the world.

Words to Understand

freelance: a person who does not work full-time for a company, but is paid for each piece of work

photo editor: the staff person at a periodical who selects which images from photographers are used in the publication

proximity: nearness

string: in sports language, to report on the same team on a regular basis; the noun would be "stringer"

Getting Started

CHAPTER 1

Sports fans have a huge appetite for information about their favorite teams and athletes. Every season is a story, or a collection of stories. The teams and players are the characters in those stories. It is the job of sportswriters and sports photographers to tell those tales.

Sportswriters and sports photographers are present at every major, and most minor, sporting events. Writers usually work in a press box or press row, while photographers are positioned as close to the action as possible. Their jobs are similar: to inform and entertain their audience.

Although they use different tools to pursue their crafts, the jobs of sportswriters and sports photographers are similar. You rarely see a story without an accompanying photo, and most photographs need a caption to help explain them. Good sportswriters and photographers reveal facts and insights about teams, players, and anyone else involved in sports that their audience may never have seen without them.

Getting Inside the Games

The digital age has changed both professions dramatically. Digital cameras allow anyone to be a sports photographer, if not necessarily as talented as a professional.

"Digital cameras have made it possible for anyone to take an ordinary sports photo," says Matt Cashore, "but it is still difficult to shoot an extraordinary sports photo."

Likewise, the Internet allows anyone to write about sports (often for free) and to potentially have as large an audience as *Sports Illustrated* or *The New York Times*. There are more opportunities, but there is also more competition.

Sports reporting and sports photography can be plenty of fun because there is nothing routine about it.

At this rally-car race in Europe, photographers take a big chance to get the action shot their editors want.

The games, the players, and the circumstances are ever-changing. Writers and "shooters," as photographers are sometimes called, might travel around the country or the world. It's an exciting ride.

If there is one thing any young sportswriter must get used to, it is that the athletes you may have once worshipped are rarely happy to see you. On the other hand, sports photographers are often welcomed because most sports figures love to be photographed. Both jobs put you in close **proximity** to some of the greatest athletes and sports events of your generation. It's a pretty cool feeling to be standing just a few feet away from a game-winning touchdown or shot that fans will be talking about for decades. It's an even cooler feeling to be able to share that moment with the masses through your words or photography. The path to either career begins as early as you want it to.

Education

It's never too early to develop a talent for writing. When *Sports Illustrated* senior writer Steve Rushin was in elementary school, he used to play his brothers in table tennis or pick-up basketball. Then he would write mock news stories about the games as if he were writing about his beloved Minnesota Vikings. That may be a little extreme, but a passion for both sports and for

writing—and not just one or the other—is what a budding sportswriter should possess.

When Maureen Cavanaugh, a former deputy **photo editor** at *Sports Illustrated*, was in grade school, she used to take pictures for a free newspaper that she and her two friends published. They called it the *Northwood Times*, after the street on which they lived, and distributed it to neighbors. A childhood hobby can turn into a career.

Most high schools have a newspaper and a yearbook where you can pursue an interest in sportswriting or photography. More than anything, though, you should pursue an interest in curiosity.

"My entire act," comedian Jerry Seinfeld once said, "is about paying attention." That holds true for writers and photographers as well. It sounds simple, but these words of advice must be heeded: Don't just see, observe; don't just hear, listen. A sports photographer's "eye," his uncanny ability to take unique shots that other photographers never seem to capture, is not a technical skill. It's a skill that he hones from the way he views the world.

"All good photographers are curious people," says Cashore, and the same is true for writers.

Learning the Games

If you want to write about sports, you should learn as much about them as possible, or at least educate yourself thoroughly about one or two sports that most interest you. Read up and watch documentaries about a sport's history. ESPN's *30 for 30* series, for example, features terrific mini-history lessons.

Understand the rules of your sport. Knowing how the games are supposed to be played will help you report what you see. It will also help you speak the same sports language as the athletes and coaches you'll interview.

While it's not necessary, it never hurts to have some experience playing sports, even if you are not going to be a star like Tom Brady or Kevin Durant. *Sports Illustrated* college football writer Andy Staples was a walk-on offensive lineman for the University of Florida Gators. That experience helps Andy to

Hall of Fame writer Peter Gammons (left) has made the study of baseball and its people his life's work.

Joe Robbins has been covering sports with his cameras since he was in high school. Early enthusiasm led to a career.

understand both the point of view of the athlete and the fan. His experience as a player helps him be a better reporter.

On the other hand, if all you know about is sports, your perspective will be too narrow. The more you know about history, or literature, or science, or anything, the better writer you will be. Knowledge is your foundation.

High school is a time to explore many interests. Don't worry about whether or not you are good enough to write or take pictures for the school yearbook or newspaper. Your enthusiasm and willingness to learn is all that is required.

Joe Robbins, a **freelance** photographer who also works for Getty Images, was once just a kid whose parents had season tickets to Cincinnati Bengals' games. When he was in high school, his parents bought him a camera for Christmas.

"I began taking my own shots at games and then looking at magazines that had sports photographs," Robbins says. "When I learned to develop film, when I saw the print first appear from a blank piece of paper, I was hooked."

"I started out shooting mostly landscape shots or photos of fellow students," says Cashore. "But it was the repetition, gaining familiarity with my equipment and the process, that was so invaluable."

Getting a Leg Up

What might you do in high school and college besides writing for your school's newspaper?

"Write as much as you can for anyone who will print your stuff, even for free," says *Sports Illustrated* writer Brian Hamilton. "Pitch unique feature ideas about local high schools or colleges that no one pays much attention to. Offer to **string** [cover] games for out-of-town newspapers or Web sites that maybe can't afford to send writers to the area."

Internships are unpaid, on-the-job learning opportunities. They are valuable for two reasons. First, they provide a hands-on glimpse of what the real world is all about. Second, you will meet people who may be in a position to offer you a job, or who may refer you to someone else who is looking for a young, eager writer or photographer.

My Story

When I was just out of college, I taught high school chemistry in Santa Fe, New Mexico. One day, I entered the offices of the local newspaper, the *Santa Fe New Mexican*, and offered to cover—for free—any games they needed covered. The editor assigned me high school girls' basketball, which was terrific. The level of the sport is not important when you are starting out. What is important is learning how to cover a game and interview people, to tell a story that is concise and interesting. It's not as easy as it looks.—J.W.

"My first job was an eight-week internship at *ESPN The Magazine*," says FOX Sports senior writer Stewart Mandel. "I went to a job fair and met an editor from a different magazine, but she saw that I had a sports background and was nice enough to put me in contact with a friend of hers from ESPN."

"Get as immersed in the sports world, or in your own local sports world, as possible," says FOX Sports senior college football writer Bruce Feldman. "Know as much as you can about the sport you hope to cover, but also meet people in the business and try to develop those relationships. That's key, relationships. It'll be key if you want to work as a reporter, and it's a big help for you to navigate the business."

Whether you want to be a writer or a photographer, you can always launch your own Web site. As a photographer, you could post photos that you take. As a writer, you could turn a blog into your own personal periodical. Even if your blog or Web site is seen by no one other than family or friends, it is a way for you to develop your style. It's also your own personal portfolio of material. If you have the time and dedication, it can be a lot of fun, too.

Classwork Options

Should you major in journalism? You can, but in this journalist's opinion, your time would be better spent learning more about a field that has its own base of information. Major in English to learn about Shakespeare or in finance to learn how the stock market operates. Study biology to understand how the body works or to find out about genetics. The more general knowledge you have and the more you can explore the world outside of sports, the better you will be at connecting those

Doing excellent work in English, communications, or any class that values writing will help your career.

An excellent way to gain experience is to work for campus publications; pictured is the Georgetown University newspaper office.

worlds to the games and the people you love to cover.

It's certainly a good idea to take classes that help you become a better writer, too. Most liberal arts courses or majors (English or history, for example) will be valuable. You can take many kinds of writing courses. If you want to be a sports photographer but have no background in photography, certainly you should take photography classes.

As a college undergraduate, nothing is more valuable than working on the school paper or yearbook. As a budding sportswriter, getting a "beat" (covering a particular team or sport) will teach you the nitty-gritty of the job. Nothing beats experience, and at the college level you are interviewing athletes who are also classmates. College coaches are almost always helpful and understanding because they are aware that you are doing this in your spare time, trying to see if it is a career that you want to pursue. They usually respect that.

Cashore arrived at Notre Dame as a college freshman in 1990 and immediately joined the school's yearbook staff. "I'd been hooked on photography since minute one back in high school," he says. "I can trace a direct line from the job I have now back to joining the yearbook as a freshman."

(Author's note: While I personally don't advise majoring in journalism—and Cashore advises against majoring in photography—studying the topic in graduate school is a great option. There are a number of schools that offer one-year,

If you choose to go the "J School" route, the Graduate School of Journalism at Columbia University is one of the best training grounds in the nation.

postgraduate journalism programs. I highly recommend this, especially if you are unable to land a job or internship straight out of college. Three of the best journalism schools, or "J Schools," as they are known, are at the University of Missouri, Columbia University in New York, and the Medill School of Journalism at Northwestern University. By having this master's degree in journalism with your general studies and your interest in sports, you'll have the triple play you need for a career as a journalist.)

However, nothing can replace enthusiasm and commitment. Once, a young wannabe sportswriter attended a career seminar where the speaker was a veteran member of *Sports Illustrated* who advised that the most important thing for people starting out was "to get your foot in the door."

The wannabe sportswriter went home, made a plaster cast of his foot, and then sent it by overnight mail to the speaker. He included a note that read, "At least I got my foot in the door."

He got hired.

Text-Dependent Questions

1. Does the author of this book recommend majoring in journalism?

2. Name at least one personality trait that a good sports journalist should have.

3. What school publications are good training grounds for photographers?

Research Project

Find a Web site that covers your local town or city and look at their high school sports reporting. What sports are not being covered? Find a smaller sport and report on an event to practice your "game reporting."

Words to Understand

credential: a document that gives the holder permission to take part in an event in a way not open to the public

deft: clever and skillful

fact-checkers: people who read a writer's work and make sure that all dates, numbers, spellings, facts, and more are correct

odyssey: a long trip to a distant place that often takes a lot of twists and turns

transcribed: typed or wrote out the words from a recording

Hard at Work

CHAPTER
2

Sportswriting and sports photography can take you anywhere on the planet. In 2012, Tim Crothers, a former *Sports Illustrated* writer who is now an author, was tipped off about a young female chess prodigy living in poverty in Africa. Soon, Crothers found himself on an odyssey that took him from his home in North Carolina to Kampala, the capital of Uganda, and ultimately to a chess tournament in Siberia.

Crothers had the time of his life, but the adventure had its drawbacks. "The airline lost my luggage," he recalls. "I spent an entire week in the frigid Russian wilderness with only the clothes I had worn on the flight."

Matt Cashore, the photographer at the University of Notre Dame, stood at midfield moments before kickoff of the Nevada versus Notre Dame game in 2009 in order to take a panoramic, 360-degree shot of the teams and fans inside Notre Dame

Stadium. Both teams had already taken the field and there stood Cashore, camera in hand, on the 50-yard line.

"I thought to myself, 'I'm literally holding up this game for everyone,'" says Cashore.

A Changing Job Market

Not every assignment is as dramatic as those two. The truth is that you will probably have to work a few years before such adventures fall into your lap. Before you ever reach Siberia or, as this writer once did, Antarctica, you will spend hundreds of hours in locker rooms, in press boxes, and on the Internet. That's the reality of the job.

Legendary former college basketball coach Bobby Knight, who was no fan of sportswriters, used to love to demean the career by saying, "Most of us learned to read and write by third grade."

True, but how to do it well? The best place to begin a sportswriting career is anywhere you can.

"My first 'kinda real' job was as an editorial assistant-slash-writer at *College & Pro Football Newsweekly* in Long Island," says FOX Sports senior writer Bruce Feldman. "I made five dollars an hour and worked thirty hours a week, all on the weekends, and I stayed at a relative's home."

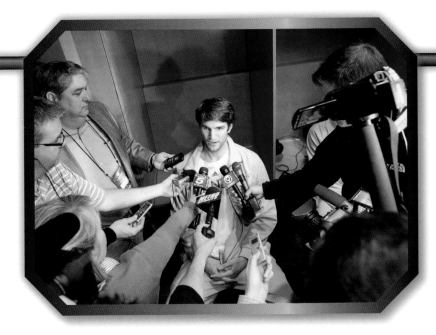

Sports reporters should expect to be in a crowd after big events, especially when trying to get a quote from one of the stars.

How did Feldman land that job? "I made about two hundred phone calls to any sports publication I could find that was looking for cheap help," he says.

Cashore began by sending his pictures to photo editors at newspapers that he admired or wanted to work for. "I asked them to take a look at my photos and give me feedback," says Cashore. "Not everyone told me things I wanted to hear, but I learned a lot. Also, through that, I made connections and eventually landed assignments."

The job landscape has changed greatly in just the past decade. Entry-level jobs for sportswriters used to be as stringers, or reporters who cover individual games or events, or as **fact-checkers** at magazines. Some of the biggest names at *Sports Illustrated*, such as senior writer Steve Rushin and the magazine's

At some events, photographers are required to remain in only a few areas. That makes it more of a challenge to find a unique shot that stands out from the pack.

top two editors, Chris Stone and Jon Wertheim, started out as fact-checkers. However, most of those jobs have disappeared as the Internet has taken over. The U.S. Bureau of Labor Statistics predicts only a tiny growth in the number of jobs in the field. That follows a decade of steady decline in the need for full-time sports journalists.

Sports photography is also a very tough nut to crack. As Cashore noted, taking pictures is easier than ever. Fewer and fewer magazines and newspapers have paid photographers, as they rely on freelancers.

The Working Writer

You must be a self-starter. Whether you are covering a particular team or a sport or are simply a freelancer, remember that no publication ever has too many good story ideas. Half the job is the ability to come up with creative and intriguing story ideas.

The other half is to execute them. (Do you want a "third half"? That would be making sure you file those stories before your deadline!)

A pro tip: If you want to endear yourself to an editor, make her job easier by doing all of the above.

When Donald Katz was a relative unknown, he heard about a strange competition in Yorkshire, England. Apparently, local people stuffed live ferrets down their trousers and saw who could tolerate the...discomfort the longest. Katz pitched the idea to an editor at *Outside* magazine, who took a chance on him and sent him to Yorkshire. The story became a classic because not only was it an original idea, but Katz handled it with a **deft**, understated touch.

Feature stories, or "long-form pieces" as they are now often called, involve great commitments in terms of time and effort. You may reach out to a dozen or even two dozen people for interviews. You will find that the more people you interview, the easier the story is to write.

"If you have writer's block," says former *Sports Illustrated* senior writer William Nack, referring to that dreadful feeling when you have no idea what to type, "that just means that you need to go out and do more reporting."

Jay Glazer started out in the early 1990s working for an NFL fan magazine that kept tabs on the New York Giants. There were weeks when Glazer would not get paid. Even when he did get paid, his salary barely covered bus fare.

"I asked myself, 'How can I stand out among the other reporters?'" says Glazer. The first thing he did was make sure that he was always the last writer to leave the practice facility. He tried to talk to every player he could as they walked out to their car.

"My idea was that an NFL player probably worked very hard to get where he is," says Glazer, who is now well-known as a FOX Sports NFL "insider." "So I wanted the Giants to see that I worked hard, too. I hoped that they'd respect that and maybe they'd be more willing to talk to me than to another writer."

Today, Glazer is a celebrity himself, and quite wealthy. Still, during football season, he spends Saturdays making phone calls to all 32 NFL teams.

"My talent," Glazer says, "is brokering information."

No matter for whom she writes, a sportswriter's "office" is really her laptop computer and her cell phone (and, occasionally, a coffee shop that has wi-fi). A photographer's office is his garage and the trunk of his car. If you cover a particular team, you are expected to cover press conferences and games and to be there whenever that team extends "media availability" (i.e., an opportunity to interview players and coaches).

Contrary to popular opinion, a media **credential** (i.e., "press pass") is not like a passport. You are not given a credential that allows you free access to any sporting event. Most media credentials must be applied for on an event-by-event basis. If you cover one team or sport throughout a season, you may be

A press conference after an event ensures that everyone has a chance to hear from the winner.

given a season pass. Also, a credential is not a ticket; you cannot give it away or sell it to someone else.

No one starts out as a sports columnist. Most of the time writers begin as beat writers, which is excellent training, but also demanding. It's sort of like boot camp. As a beat writer, you will likely cover a single team. Your job is to gather information and to break news—for example, a major trade or a coach being fired—before any of the other reporters on the beat do so. It is a round-the-clock job, and there is plenty of stress.

Sportswriting calls for interviewing people. During the interviews, you take notes or record the entire interview. Once recorded, interviews must be **transcribed**, which means typed or written out. This is a time-consuming and unglamorous aspect of the job. Once the interviews are done, the writing can begin.

Along the way, interesting things can happen. Feldman fondly recalls a road trip he took with Ed Orgeron, who was then the head football coach at the University of Mississippi.

"So we're driving in Coach Orgeron's Hummer on the way to the Memphis airport," says Feldman. "It's normally a seventy-five-minute drive from Ole Miss. About ten minutes in, we stop at a convenience store. Coach buys a four-pack of Red Bull, a packet of mixed nuts, and some pork rinds. In the fifty minutes it takes him to drive to the airport, he sizes up his entire recruiting class, the strengths and weaknesses of every staffer he had, tells a great old Jimmy Johnson story . . . and finishes all four Red Bulls and the pork rinds."

Shooting for a Living

Photographers are very rarely fully employed by a single media outlet anymore. Most of them work as freelancers, and they may have contracts with a photo service, such as Getty Images. In fact, in 2015, *Sports Illustrated* fired all of its full-time staff photographers. The magazine will continue to use photography, of course, but no one will be paid year round to take those pictures.

Because Cashore is Notre Dame's official photographer, he has found himself on the sidelines of national championship football games, but also in a room in the Vatican with the university's president and Pope Francis.

"It's never boring," says Cashore, "but the reality is that photographers have to be prepared to work anywhere under any conditions. And many sports photographers supplement their income by being other types of photographers. I know some who are even wedding photographers."

Sports photography is not a team sport. Photographers are basically on their own at most events.

"You have to be more like [golfer] Tiger Woods than [NBA star] Tim Duncan," says Cashore.

Sportswriters build relationships, which helps them to build a network of sources. Photographers, however, are lone wolves. They are judged by the quality of their photos and how resourceful they are. "I had to shoot a football game in Los Angeles," says Cashore, "and I didn't bring any rain gear.

Just like the players, photographers have to battle the elements, making sure to protect gear that can be worth thousands of dollars.

Of course, it rained. So I had to run to a grocery store and buy turkey-baster bags to put over my camera."

Like the athletes they cover, photographers must battle the elements to do their job. Like those athletes, too, their bosses won't listen to any excuses about the weather. The "shooters" have the best seats in the house, but they are also among the hardest-working people in the stadium.

Text-Dependent Questions

1. What does a press pass allow a writer or photographer to do?

2. What team did Jay Glazer first cover before he became a nationally famous writer?

3. What magazine fired all its staff photographers in 2015?

Research Project

Next time you watch a sports event on TV or you attend one in person, watch the photographers as much as you can. How do they move around the court or the field? How do they watch the action—through their lenses, or their eyes, or both? What hazards do they have to watch out for as they work?

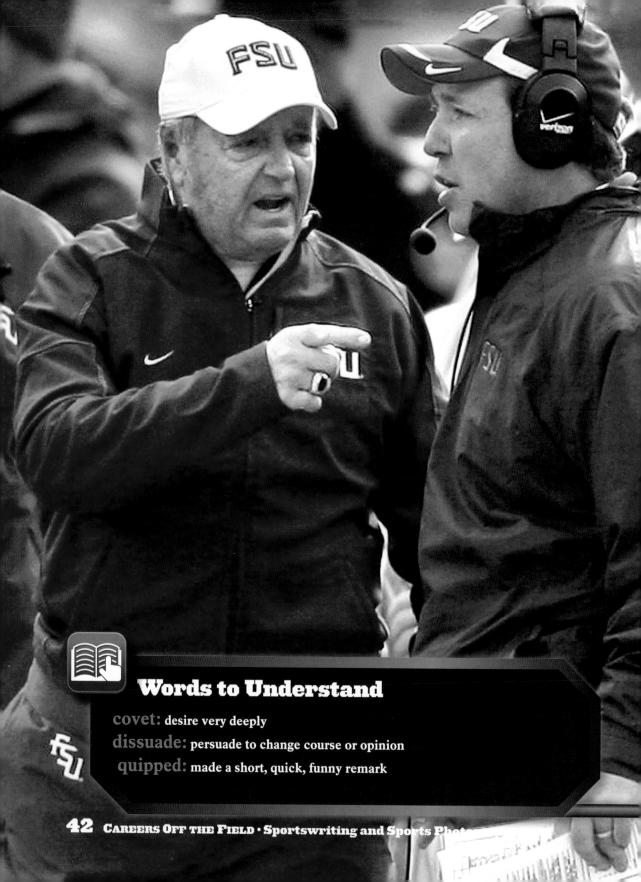

Words to Understand

covet: desire very deeply

dissuade: persuade to change course or opinion

quipped: made a short, quick, funny remark

Realities of the Workplace

Standing in front of a roomful of sportswriters, former Florida State football coach Bobby Bowden, then in his sixties, was asked what kept him motivated. "Winning national championships," answered Bowden (left), who one day earlier had led the Seminoles to victory and the national title in the 1994 Orange Bowl. "What keeps you guys motivated in your career?"

At that, Peter Vecsey, a well-respected columnist at *The New York Times*, **quipped**, "Frequent flier miles."

The room burst into laughter.

Tough Competition

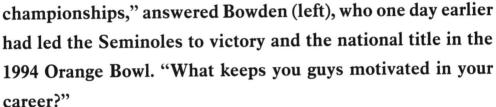

The path of a sportswriter or sports photographer involves lots of airports, rental cars, and hotels. You may spend Christmas or Thanksgiving far from home and family. There's always the chance that, through no fault of your own, your job may cease to exist. While your duties often involve interviewing or taking photos of millionaires, you almost certainly won't become one.

While many sportswriters or sports photographers would advise you not to follow their career path, those same people would never abandon it. Every job has its pitfalls, but most sportswriters and photographers enjoy what they do too much to consider leaving.

"The two reasons to get into this business," says photographer Joe Robbins, "is, one, you want to tell stories in a visual way. Two, it beats working for a living."

The first hurdle you will encounter as you embark on a career in sportswriting or photography is people like yourself. Lots of young people **covet** a career in sports. It looks like fun, right? However, when there are far more job applicants than there are jobs, an employer can offer that job at a lower salary, or even for no salary.

Also, the Internet has changed everything. ESPN's Bill Simmons is the greatest individual media success story of the past two decades, if not all-time. Yet, to achieve the greatness that Simmons has, including a salary that reportedly pays him a few million dollars per year, he was willing to write a blog for free for five years. Simmons supported himself as a bartender.

"When I started out at the *Seymour Tribune* in Indiana, the salary was under $20,000 a year," says photographer Joe Robbins. While Robbins is talking about the 1990s, that is still a low full-time salary.

It is almost unheard-of for a sportswriter or photographer, even those with master's degrees from journalism schools, to be high earners while in their twenties. Do yourself the favor of not worrying too much about salary in those years. Instead, focus on developing your skills.

"When I began freelancing," says Robbins, "I worked on 'spec.' That means I only got paid if they used my photos in a newspaper or some other publication. Some games I never got paid for. But the more photos I shot, the better I got. Once my photos started being used, I could afford better equipment, and that helped me to sell even more photos."

Today, competition is fierce as people struggle to get the shot.

Sports Wait for No One

Sports do not take holidays, which means that sometimes you will not, either. The NBA staged five games on Christmas Day of 2014, and the NFL played three on Thanksgiving the month before. Someone has to cover those events.

In 2013, Notre Dame basketball player Jerian Grant was suspended from school for one semester, with the announcement being made on the Saturday before Christmas. Beat writers who covered the team and probably had put off Christmas shopping until that weekend found themselves scurrying to gather news, phoning sources, and feeling as if the Grinch had stolen their holiday, too.

"It comes with the territory," says Pete Sampson, who covers Notre Dame sports for Rivals.com. "But you're always on call when you have a beat. The news never waits for when it's convenient."

"It helps to have the most understanding spouse in the

NBA writers, just like NBA cheerleaders, often can expect to work on Christmas Day.

world," says Cashore, who is married and has a young daughter. "A couple of years ago, I got four days' notice that I was going to South Africa for a week. Great for me, sure. But my wife and I had to scramble for day care and stuff like that. It's as if I'm Seal Team Six in terms of being deployed, and my wife has to roll with that."

Also, you may have noticed that most sporting events do not take place between the "normal" business hours of nine A.M. and five P.M., Monday through Friday. Sportswriters and sports photographers work many nights and weekends, when the rest of the world is off. Sure, it is fun to attend the games, but you are working.

At times it may feel as if you exist in an opposite world from most people you know. You may have Monday off, but you are working Saturday. You're free all afternoon, but you'll be covering a night game and have a tight midnight deadline to file your story.

"People have no understanding of the process," says Tim Prister, who has covered Notre Dame football for roughly three decades. "On a typical Saturday, for a game that lasts a little more than three hours, it's a twelve-hour day. That's just the reality."

Travel, too, is a lot like ice cream: It is possible to have too much of a good thing. Talk to any sportswriter or sports photographer who has been in the business for 20 years. Every one of them has a story about waking up in a hotel room and having no idea where they are, or about exiting an arena and suddenly remembering that they have no idea where they parked their rental car—or what color it is.

A Tough Road Ahead

"Job security is terrible," says Cashore. "It used to be that the most common starting spot for a photographer or writer was a small-town newspaper, but they're all going out of business."

That sounds depressing, but you cannot let it **dissuade** you too much. Journalism is undergoing its most radical change perhaps since the invention of the typewriter in 1874. The industry is not dying; it's just still in the process of figuring out how to distribute its product and be profitable in a new landscape in which the Internet allows consumers to get stories and photos for free.

Still, the realities must be faced. For one thing, travel budgets have been drastically reduced. I found a story that I wanted to do in a remote part of Canada in the summer of 2014.

My editors loved the idea, but could not afford to pay the entire cost of the trip. So I spent the equivalent of a week's salary just to do the story.

That's not a very smart long-term business plan.

As for full-time benefits, such as health care, that, too, is becoming a luxury. Many famous news outlets no longer offer such benefits to new hires. For example, many of the writers at ESPN.com, names that you may recognize from reading them online, are forced to work less than 30 weeks per year. Why? It allows ESPN to not count them as full-time employees under the law, which allows them not to provide benefits.

As in all things, it helps to have a sense of humor. To cover a major sports team is to know the feeling, for example, of a famous athlete having no desire to speak with you. You may approach him as politely as possible, and he may completely ignore you, or he may talk to you without even looking you in the eye. One writer reports how a certain member of the New York Mets enjoyed walking past reporters and breaking wind where they stood.

These are "war stories" that you can save and share with your colleagues. If you are worried about the people you cover liking you, sportswriting is the wrong career to pursue. Your only concern is that they respect the way you go about doing your job.

Keeping good relations with fellow photographers in tight sideline spaces can be a challenge.

You will learn that you will never, ever please everyone. If your editor likes your story, there is an excellent chance that someone profiled in the story will not like the way in which they were portrayed. No one will ever call to complain that you portrayed them inaccurately if your story makes them appear better than they actually are. Make sure that the facts are on your side and be fair. You may still get complaints from readers or the subjects themselves, but that is part of being a journalist.

Sometimes, even your own colleagues can be the problem. "All photographers are egomaniacs," says Cashore, "and most of the most successful ones are [unprintable]. You have to roll with it. I try to remain Zen. If, for example, a guy intentionally gets in the way of my shot during a game, I used to yell at him. Now I stay calm and remind myself that next time, he may be getting in the way of another photographer's shot, which helps me out."

Most of all, remember that most people would love to be able to write about or photograph sports for a living. "I was nineteen years old, it was summertime, and I was standing in the kitchen complaining about something," recalls Bruce Feldman of FOX Sports. "It was ninety degrees out, and we had two men in the backyard working on our septic tank. My mom, without looking up, said, 'Go outside and see if the men want anything to drink.' I'll never forget that. It was her way of telling me, 'That's real work.'

"Sure, there are times when I feel as if I travel too much and am away from my family, or the press box food is not what I'd like. But I get to watch games and tell stories for a living. I'm a lucky guy."

Text-Dependent Questions

1. What is one drawback of the travel that is part of sports journalism?

2. What is the biggest way the Internet has affected sports journalism?

3. Where did the author go for a story even after his editors didn't want to pay for his entire trip?

Research Project

Start a blog about your favorite sports team, even if it's just on your own computer, not on a Web site. Show it to your family and friends, and ask them to give you an honest opinion. Did they enjoy reading it? What did you do well? What do you need to work on?

Words to Understand

enticing: luring, persuading, or convincing

lede: journalism's spelling of the word "lead," meaning the first few sentences or paragraph of a story

gamer: in this case, a write-up of a game

The Nitty-Gritty

The next time you attend a major sports event, train your eyes on a photographer during a time-out or between innings. More than likely, that shooter will be staring intently into his display window. If you look closely, his fingers will be manipulating a button or two on the camera.

The photographer is "chimping," which is a term in the business for editing photos on the spot. (Eric Isaacs demonstrates at left.) In today's sports world, photographers do not have the luxury of waiting for slides to come back from a developer to see what they've got. Their editors want the pictures immediately, often even before the game is over.

Upstairs in the press box, Brian Hamilton of *Sports Illustrated* stares at a blank screen. The football game he is covering has just ended and now he must file (that is, "write") his game story, or "**gamer**." The question is: how to begin? An editor in New York City waits for his story, and the deadline clock is ticking. Hamilton can't waste any time; he has to start writing—now.

Writers file. Photographers shoot. What, though, do they produce, and how do they do it?

Building a Story

Let's begin with writers and the types of stories they file. Before you write any story of any length, this is the most important thing to remember: Your story should always answer these six questions: Who? What? Where? When? Why? and How? Those six questions, and the answers to them, are your guide.

The most basic story is a game story, or "gamer." A game story tells the story of a live event, so it is no different than describing an incident to your friends. Who won (and who lost)? What were they playing?

The highlight of any game or event story is letting fans know who won.

Where did it take place, and when? Why were the Warriors able to beat the Lakers? (Better outside shooting?) How did they do it? (By feeding Klay Thompson and Stephen Curry?) Gamers need to be written quickly right after an event. A gamer that is several days old is out of date.

A "feature" is a story, normally of greater length, that is not event-related. It may be a profile of an athlete or a coach. It may be a story that examines an issue, such as concussions in sports. Features, unlike gamers, are not always time-sensitive. You will have more time to report them, and the difference in the quality of your writing should reflect that. Feature stories can be read almost at any time, while a gamer needs to be read at once. Think of gamers as fast food and features as fine dining.

Your story, whether it is a gamer or feature, begins with the "lead" (also spelled as "lede," to avoid confusion), which is its first sentence or first few sentences. A good lede informs the reader of the story's essential facts or argument, while **enticing** the reader to continue reading further. The golden rule for writing a lede? Capture the audience's attention.

Most stories, but particularly news stories and gamers, employ two other parts of good journalism: the "inverted pyramid" and the "nut graf." Picture a pyramid upside down.

It is broader at the top and pointy at the bottom. Think of your story that way. Begin with a broad overview of what you are about to discuss (e.g., "Soccer is a more popular youth sport than baseball"), then dive into details. The inverted pyramid is the structure of your story. The more important parts of the story are at the start, with less important details coming later.

The term "nut graf" is derived from "nutshell paragraph." In other words, can you describe what your story is about in, as they say, "a nutshell"? That's another way of saying, "as briefly as possible" or "get to the point." The "nut graf" is usually the second or third paragraph. Think of it as the summary, in a sentence or two, of what your story is all about.

Interview Tips

Journalists interview people. Good journalists interview lots of people, then they interview even more. How exactly do you interview someone? Every interview situation is different, but here are a few basic tips. Remember that just as many interviews are now conducted over the phone as they are in person. You can even try email interviews.

First, think like a five-year-old. Be curious and do not obsess too much about whether or not your question is rude.

There's a nice way to ask a question that the person whom you are interviewing may be uncomfortable answering. Again, watch how a five-year-old does it: Ask it as directly as possible.

In short, the longer the question, the worse the answer. The shorter the question, the better. Your role in an interview is to listen.

Carry a recording device—and always test it before the interview—and also a notepad. You don't need to transcribe every

A small, reliable recording device makes sportswriting easier. Don't forget fresh batteries!

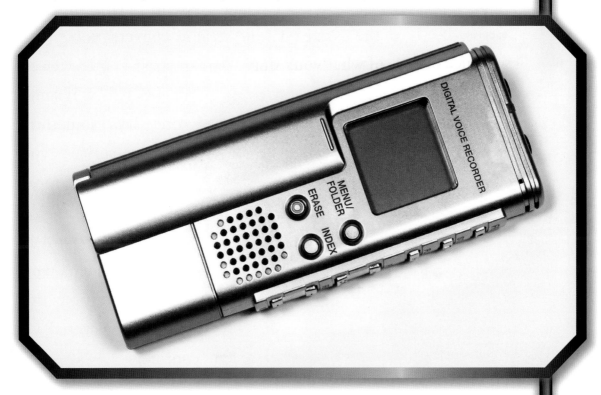

word of the interview, but you may want to jot down some of the more memorable quotes. Sometimes just writing a few key words (nouns and verbs) will help you remember what the person said. It's also a good backup in case the recording fails.

A good interviewer pays close attention to what his subject is saying. Make sure to listen and not just to wait to ask questions.

Depending on how much time you have, an interview should proceed like a conversation. Yes, there are questions you want to ask (Who? What? When? etc.), but let the stream of the conversation flow naturally. The very best interviewers L-I-S-T-E-N. If someone says something that surprises you, pursue that topic. Imagine how much of a payoff that will be for the reader. Avoid asking questions that can be answered yes or no.

More than 20 years ago, I was seated in the passenger seat of a car. The driver was Texas A&M football coach R.C. Slocum. At the time, his team was being investigated by the NCAA for alleged rules violations, and I asked Coach Slocum about it. I didn't ask, "Did your team break rules?" Instead, I asked him about what he thought of the investigation. Here's what he said:

"Do you remember the story of the Garden of Eden? They had two people and one rule, and they couldn't stay in line. I've got one hundred players and even more rules to follow."

I still remember that quote. It's a far better answer than "yes" or "no," and it provided readers with a glimpse of Coach Slocum's colorful personality.

Behind the Lens

Photographers have their own versions of gamers and features. Their tools are different (cameras versus laptop computers), but the two jobs are more similar than you might imagine.

When photographers are shooting "live action," or games, the priority is turning in your work as quickly as possible. Chimping, as noted earlier, is just one of many tricks of the trade professional photographers know. "Chimping allows me to run into the photo room almost as soon as the game ends," says Joe Robbins, a freelance photographer, "and download my photos without having to choose them. I've already done that [by chimping]."

Another trick for live action photos is the ideal shot. The next time you visit a Web site or pick up the sports page of a newspaper, look at the photos. Notice something that most action pictures all have in common. "Almost every good sports photo includes two things: the ball and a player's face," notes Cashore.

Photo editors also look for shots that have "peak action," says Robbins. "That's how they refer to a great action shot. Lots of motion, bodies in extraordinary positions, people jumping high."

A good sports photographer also knows the game he is covering. Being able to read the action and predict what is coming might mean being ready for the perfect photo before the competition. That might mean moving to a different position depending on the game situation, or switching to a different lens.

One key word to remember for live-action photography is focus. Of course, your camera must be in focus or the shot is worthless. However, the photographer must remain focused as well. Be aware of the situation: It's third-and-long so the quarterback is likely going to drop back to pass. Be aware of the conditions. Is it about to rain? Is the wind picking up?

"You have to remain focused," says Cashore. "They don't

replay game-winning touchdowns or baskets. You only get one shot at it."

Whether a story is brief or long, and whether it is told through words or photos, the job of the writers and the photographers essentially never changes. Their purpose is to communicate, to inform and enlighten. Telling stories is a uniquely human trait. So that means the writer's and photographer's job, even in sports, is to provide a better understanding of what it is to be human.

Text-Dependent Questions

1. What are the six key questions for an interview?

2. What is a "nut graf"?

3. What is "chimping"?

Research Project

Attend a game and see if you can write a good game story, even without adding quotes (though see if you can get some of those, too!). Photographers should cover a game, then look for the two or three best shots. Did you get a cover shot?

Find Out More

Books

Andrews, Phil. *Sports Journalism: A Practical Introduction.*
Thousand Oaks, Ca.: SAGE Publishing, 2013.

Gisondi, Joe. *Field Guide to Covering Sports.* Washington, D.C.:
CQ Press, 2010.

Miller, Peter Read. *Peter Read Miller on Sports Photography:
A Sports Illustrated Photographer's Tips, Tricks, and More.*
San Francisco: New Riders, 2013.

Skelps, Michael. *Fearless Photographer: Sports.* Boston: Cengage,
2013.

Tate, C. Dow. *Scholastic Journalism.* Malden, Mass.:
Wiley-Blackwell, 2013.

Web Sites

contently.net/2014/04/02/resources/10-content-tips-from-sports-
journalists/
This blog for freelance writers gathers tips for making your
sports blog better.

journalism.about.com/od/SportsJournalism/a/Want-To-Get-Your-Start-
In-Sports-Journalism-Cover-The-Local-Teams.htm
A general information site with great links to how-to pages
on different types of sportswriting.

sportsjournalism.org/
Indiana University at Bloomington has an extensive site about how
its students put their education to use in the sports world.

Series Glossary of Key Terms

academic: relating to classes and studies

alumni: people who graduate from a particular college

boilerplate: a standard set of text and information that an organization puts at the end of every press release

compliance: the action of following rules

conferences: groups of schools that play each other frequently in sports

constituencies: a specific group of people related by their connection to an organization or demographic group

credential: a document that gives the holder permission to take part in an event in a way not open to the public

eligibility: a student's ability to compete in sports, based on grades or other school or NCAA requirements

entrepreneurs: people who start their own companies

freelance: a person who does not work full-time for a company, but is paid for each piece of work

gamer: in sports journalism, a write-up of a game

intercollegiate: something that takes places between two schools, such as a sporting event

internships: positions that rarely offer pay but provide on-the-job experience

objective: material written based solely on the facts of a situation

orthopedics: the branch of medicine that specializes in preventing and correcting problems with bones and muscles

recruiting: the process of finding the best athletes to play for a team

revenue: money earned from a business or event

spreadsheets: computer programs that calculate numbers and organize information in rows and columns

subjective: material written from a particular point of view, choosing facts to suit the opinion

Index

Credits

Dreamstime.com: Nils Versammen 18, Wickedgood 21, MonkeyBusiness 25, Bigapplestock 28, Jamie Roach 30, Zhukovsky 37; paparazzofamily 34, 40; Malbright 45; Natursports 50; PNeisen 54; Alysta 57. Courtesy Matt Cashore: 10, 14; Patrick Neil: 26; Mike Eliason: 58. Courtesy Joe Robbins: 22, 45, 52.

Newscom: Jon SooHoo/UPI 8; Patrick Allen 16; Bo Rader/Wichita Eagle 33; Stephen Dowell/Orlando Sentinel 42; John Angelillo/UPI 46.

About the Author

John Walters is a senior sportswriter at *Newsweek* magazine. He previously worked at NBC Sports, where he was the recipient of two Sports Emmys for Olympic coverage, and at *Sports Illustrated*. He is the author of *The Same River Twice: A Season with Geno Auriemma and the Connecticut Huskies.*